Instant Cartoons
for Church Newsletters
2

George W. Knight *Compiler*

Baker Book House
Grand Rapids, Michigan 49506

Another Handy Book of Instant Humor

Because of the very positive response to our first book of instant cartoons, we have compiled a second book for churches to use in bulletins and newsletters.

Most church newsletters tend to be a little on the stuffy side—formal and proper but lacking in humor and the lighter approach to the Christian life. Now there is a quick-and-easy remedy for that situation. To give your church members a welcome shot of laughter, select and clip these cartoons and use them as needed. All are copyright-free to local churches, so there's no need to write for permission to publish.

Three different cartoonists—Howard Stringer, Joe McKeever, and Howard Paris—contributed to this collection of Christian humor. You'll notice immediately that each has his own unique style. For best results, mix their cartoons from issue to issue of your newsletter. This will expose your church members to a continuing variety of humorous situations to help them appreciate the lighter side of their faith.

The writer of the Proverbs declared, "A merry heart doeth good like a medicine" (Proverbs 17:22a). This second book should also serve as "good medicine" by helping Christians learn to laugh at themselves a little more.

George W. Knight

About the cartoonists....

Howard Paris works out of his home studio in suburban Atlanta, Georgia. His popular cartoon "Butch" has run as a regular feature in *Home Life* for thirty years. He has had cartoons published in over 200 markets. In addition, he has four books of cartoons published.

Since 1974 Joe Neil McKeever has pastored the First Baptist Church in Columbus, Mississippi. He is syndicated by the Copley News Service of San Diego and his cartoons are seen in over a million papers each week. He has also illustrated several religious books and in 1978 drew a 28-page full-color comic book for use by Baptists in Singapore.

Howard Stringer is a drafter employed by the Kerr McGee Corporation. He lives with his family in Mustang near Oklahoma City, Oklahoma. He has had two books of cartoons published and has sold over 2000 cartoons to more than a hundred markets.

JUST THINK—BIBLE SCHOLARS A FEW THOUSAND YEARS FROM NOW WILL HAVE AN AWFUL TIME FIGURING THIS OUT!

THE REASON THEY CALL THIS THE SPACE AGE IS THERE'S SO LITTLE OF IT.

SINCE WE BROKE THE WINDOW, IT'S ONLY
RIGHT THAT WE PUT IN A NEW ONE.

THE DAWN IS BREAKING OVER YONDER
THICKET, THE RAYS OF SUNLIGHT TOUCHING
TREE AND HOUSE AND CHURCH....

THE REASON THEY CALL THIS THE SPACE
AGE IS THERE'S SO LITTLE OF IT.

JUST THINK—BIBLE SCHOLARS A FEW
THOUSAND YEARS FROM NOW WILL HAVE AN
AWFUL TIME FIGURING THIS OUT!

THE DAWN IS BREAKING OVER YONDER
THICKET, THE RAYS OF SUNLIGHT TOUCHING
TREE AND HOUSE AND CHURCH...

SINCE WE BROKE THE WINDOW, IT'S ONLY
RIGHT THAT WE PUT IN A NEW ONE.

NOT YOU TOO!

I'LL SAY ONE THING. YOU REALLY KNOW HOW TO PICK A NAME.

GEORGE, I HEAR YOU'RE TO HAVE A PART IN THE CHURCH THANKSGIVING PAGEANT.

PERHAPS I'M KEEPING YOU A LITTLE LONG THIS MORNING....

I'LL SAY ONE THING. YOU REALLY KNOW HOW
TO PICK A NAME.

NOT YOU TOO!

PERHAPS I'M KEEPING YOU A LITTLE LONG
THIS MORNING...

GEORGE, I HEAR YOU'RE TO HAVE A PART IN
THE CHURCH THANKSGIVING PAGEANT.

THE CHRISTMAS STORY WAS GOOD, BUT I'D ALREADY SEEN IT ON TV.

THE VERY IDEA—REQUESTING PRAYER FOR YOUR SICK PLANTS.

JUST GET THEIR NAMES AND ADDRESSES.
WE DON'T NEED FINGERPRINTS.

FRIENDLIEST CHURCH WE EVER VISITED.

THE VERY IDEA—REQUESTING PRAYER FOR
YOUR SICK PLANTS.

THE CHRISTMAS STORY WAS GOOD, BUT I'D
ALREADY SEEN IT ON TV.

JUST GET THEIR NAMES AND ADDRESSES.
WE DON'T NEED FINGERPRINTS.

FRIENDLIEST CHURCH WE EVER VISITED.

I HATE TO THINK I'M LOST, BUT WHERE IN
THE WORLD DID NOAH GO WITH THAT ARK?

WHY CAN'T I TAKE HER IN? YOU SAID
THERE'S A SPECIAL MOTHER'S DAY SERVICE
TODAY.

SOMETHING TELLS ME THIS IS GOING TO BE ONE OF THOSE DAYS.

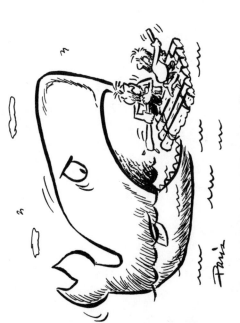

DO YOU TAKE THE JONAH-AND-THE-WHALE STORY LITERALLY?

WHY <u>CAN'T</u> I TAKE HER IN? YOU SAID
THERE'S A SPECIAL MOTHER'S DAY SERVICE
TODAY.

I HATE TO THINK I'M LOST, BUT WHERE IN
THE WORLD DID NOAH GO WITH THAT ARK?

DO YOU TAKE THE JONAH-AND-THE-WHALE
STORY LITERALLY?

SOMETHING TELLS ME THIS IS GOING TO BE
ONE OF THOSE DAYS.

WELL, IF I'M TO TEACH A CLASS OF FIVE-
YEAR-OLDS I'VE GOT TO TRIM DOWN TO FIT
THE CHAIRS.

TO SHOW YOU HOW MY LUCK IS GOING,
WHEN I CALLED DIAL-A-PRAYER I GOT THEIR
ANSWERING SERVICE.

IT ISN'T MUCH WHEN YOU CONSIDER THE GALL IT TAKES TO QUOTE YOU THAT KIND OF ESTIMATE.

YOU BE THE BAD GUY. I'LL BE THE CIRCUIT RIDER PREACHER.

TO SHOW YOU HOW MY LUCK IS GOING, WHEN I CALLED DIAL-A-PRAYER I GOT THEIR ANSWERING SERVICE.

WELL, IF I'M TO TEACH A CLASS OF FIVE-YEAR-OLDS I'VE GOT TO TRIM DOWN TO FIT THE CHAIRS.

YOU BE THE BAD GUY. I'LL BE THE CIRCUIT RIDER PREACHER.

IT ISN'T MUCH WHEN YOU CONSIDER THE GALL IT TAKES TO QUOTE YOU THAT KIND OF ESTIMATE.

I'M SORRY I'M LATE, BUT THE ZIPPER STUCK DURING MY CAMPING TRIP.

I'M WORRIED.

SORRY—NO PETS ALLOWED IN CHURCH.

I THOUGHT YOU WERE GETTING YOUR COAT
TO GO TO SUNDAY SCHOOL.

I'M WORRIED.

I'M SORRY I'M LATE, BUT THE ZIPPER STUCK
DURING MY CAMPING TRIP.

I THOUGHT YOU WERE GETTING YOUR COAT
TO GO TO SUNDAY SCHOOL.

SORRY—NO PETS ALLOWED IN CHURCH.

I THOUGHT I HEARD MUSIC.

I DO HOPE MY EXCUSE FOR BEING LATE
DOESN'T SOUND FLIMSY.

IT ISN'T THAT WE DON'T WANT YOU TO KEEP
YOUR CLASSROOM TIDY...

DON'T YOU THINK IT'S KIND OF FREDDIE TO
DRIVE YOU TO THE CHURCH BOARD
MEETING TONIGHT, DADDY?

I DO HOPE MY EXCUSE FOR BEING LATE
DOESN'T SOUND FLIMSY.

'I THOUGHT I HEARD MUSIC.

DON'T YOU THINK IT'S KIND OF FREDDIE TO
DRIVE YOU TO THE CHURCH BOARD
MEETING TONIGHT, DADDY?

IT ISN'T THAT WE DON'T WANT YOU TO KEEP
YOUR CLASSROOM TIDY...

HE DOESN'T CARRY A TUNE VERY WELL, EITHER.

ARE YOU SURE YOU LOOKED EVERYWHERE FOR THAT OTHER OFFERING PLATE?

I HAVE MY BIBLE, MY LESSON BOOK AND MY OFFERING ENVELOPE. WHAT MAKES YOU THINK I FORGOT SOMETH--

CHURCH IS A FAMILY AFFAIR WITH US. TAKES ALL THE FAMILY TO GET HIM THERE.

ARE YOU SURE YOU LOOKED EVERYWHERE
FOR THAT OTHER OFFERING PLATE?

HE DOESN'T CARRY A <u>TUNE</u> VERY WELL,
EITHER.

CHURCH IS A FAMILY AFFAIR WITH US. TAKES
ALL THE FAMILY TO GET HIM THERE.

I HAVE MY BIBLE, MY LESSON BOOK AND MY
OFFERING ENVELOPE. WHAT MAKES YOU
THINK I FORGOT SOMETH--

IT SAYS, "THE MODERN CHURCH MEMBER TENDS TO BE DISINTERESTED IN THE FINANCIAL NEEDS OF HIS CHURCH."

THIS IS MORRIS. HE LIVES IN THE CHOIR ROOM.

IT SAYS, "THE MODERN CHURCH MEMBER
TENDS TO BE DISINTERESTED IN THE
FINANCIAL NEEDS OF HIS CHURCH."

THIS IS MORRIS. HE LIVES IN THE CHOIR
ROOM.

I KNOW WE'RE PILGRIMS ON THIS EARTHLY SOD, BUT I'M ASKING GOD FOR SQUATTERS' RIGHTS ON A TWO-STORY CAPE COD, BEAUTIFULLY LANDSCAPED ON A HALF ACRE, AT EIGHT PERCENT FINANCING.

AND SUNDAY LOOKS LIKE A LOVELY DAY TO FORSAKE NOT THE ASSEMBLING OF YOURSELVES TOGETHER.

PORTIONS OF PASTOR MOSELEY'S SERMON TODAY WERE WITHOUT POWER—THE PUBLIC UTILITY HAS ISSUED A STATEMENT DENYING ALL RESPONSIBILITY.

I KNOW WE'RE PILGRIMS ON THIS EARTHLY SOD, BUT I'M ASKING GOD FOR SQUATTERS' RIGHTS ON A TWO-STORY CAPE COD, BEAUTIFULLY LANDSCAPED ON A HALF ACRE, AT EIGHT PERCENT FINANCING.

AND SUNDAY LOOKS LIKE A LOVELY DAY TO FORSAKE NOT THE ASSEMBLING OF YOURSELVES TOGETHER.

PORTIONS OF PASTOR MOSELEY'S SERMON TODAY WERE WITHOUT POWER—THE PUBLIC UTILITY HAS ISSUED A STATEMENT DENYING ALL RESPONSIBILITY.

I DON'T USE IT MUCH—JUST ADD A LITTLE TO MY OWN IDEAS TO MAKE THEM GO FARTHER.

I THOUGHT BOB WAS GOING TO BE HERE.

LOOK, HON—THIS MEDICAL REPORT SAYS
MOST AMERICAN MEN PUSH THEMSELVES
TOO HARD AND NEED TO SLOW DOWN.

THE PREACHERS ARE JUST HAVING
COFFEE—AND SWAPPING COMBAT STORIES.

I THOUGHT BOB WAS GOING TO BE HERE.

I DON'T USE IT MUCH—JUST ADD A LITTLE TO MY OWN IDEAS TO MAKE THEM GO FARTHER.

THE PREACHERS ARE JUST HAVING COFFEE—AND SWAPPING COMBAT STORIES.

LOOK, HON—THIS MEDICAL REPORT SAYS MOST AMERICAN MEN PUSH THEMSELVES TOO HARD AND NEED TO SLOW DOWN.

I CERTAINLY AM INTERESTED IN THE BUILDING FUND, PASTOR—IN FACT, JUST LAST NIGHT I WAS PRAYING FOR ONE OF THOSE MILLIONAIRES TO JOIN OUR CHURCH!

YOU REALLY HELPED MAKE THE REVIVAL A SUCCESS!—HOW WAS YOUR TRIP OUT OF TOWN?

THERE'S NOTHING WRONG WITH THE SOAPS
THAT A LITTLE SOAP COULDN'T FIX.

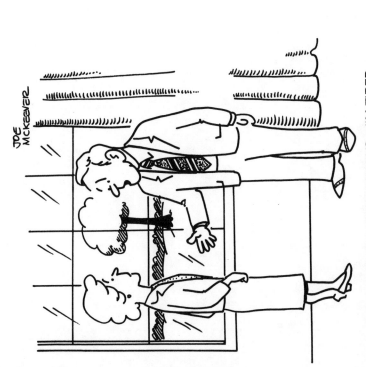

I'VE DECIDED TO MEND MY WAYS—I'M TIRED
OF PRAYING UNDER AN ASSUMED NAME.

YOU REALLY HELPED MAKE THE REVIVAL A SUCCESS!—HOW WAS YOUR TRIP OUT OF TOWN?

I CERTAINLY AM INTERESTED IN THE BUILDING FUND, PASTOR—IN FACT, JUST LAST NIGHT I WAS PRAYING FOR ONE OF THOSE MILLIONAIRES TO JOIN OUR CHURCH!

I'VE DECIDED TO MEND MY WAYS—I'M TIRED OF PRAYING UNDER AN ASSUMED NAME.

THERE'S NOTHING WRONG WITH THE SOAPS THAT A LITTLE SOAP COULDN'T FIX.

A SQUADRON OF ALIEN STARSHIPS IS THREATENING OUR CIVILIZATION AND YOU TELL ME TO GO HOME AND RAKE THE LEAVES!

NOW I KNOW WHY I DIDN'T ENJOY SMOKING—I NEVER WAS DRESSED FOR IT.

AND ANOTHER THING, LAST SUNDAY'S SERMON NEEDS A COMPLETE OVERHAUL.

BOB IS THE ASSISTANT PASTOR—MR. HENDERSON IS THE <u>PRIME MINISTER</u>.

NOW I KNOW WHY I DIDN'T ENJOY SMOKING—I NEVER WAS DRESSED FOR IT.

A SQUADRON OF ALIEN STARSHIPS IS THREATENING OUR CIVILIZATION AND YOU TELL ME TO GO HOME AND RAKE THE LEAVES!

BOB IS THE ASSISTANT PASTOR—MR. HENDERSON IS THE <u>PRIME MINISTER</u>.

AND ANOTHER THING, LAST SUNDAY'S SERMON NEEDS A COMPLETE OVERHAUL.

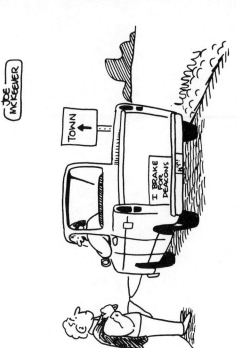

MAKE A DEAL WITH YOU, PASTOR—I'LL GIVE
YOU A LIFT TODAY AND YOU GIVE ME ONE
SUNDAY.

IT'S ELEVEN O'CLOCK, SUNDAY MORNING—
DO YOU KNOW WHERE YOUR CHURCH IS?

PLEASE STAY TUNED. THE PASTOR HAS LOST HIS PLACE IN THE SERMON. WE EXPECT HIM TO RECOVER MOMENTARILY.

THINK HE KNOWS SOMETHING?

IT'S ELEVEN O'CLOCK, SUNDAY MORNING—
DO YOU KNOW WHERE YOUR CHURCH IS?

MAKE A DEAL WITH YOU, PASTOR—I'LL GIVE
YOU A LIFT TODAY AND YOU GIVE ME ONE
SUNDAY.

THINK HE KNOWS SOMETHING?

PLEASE STAY TUNED. THE PASTOR HAS LOST
HIS PLACE IN THE SERMON. WE EXPECT HIM
TO RECOVER MOMENTARILY.

NOT ONLY IS HE A GREAT P... RECENT SERMON O... PRINTED IN THE C...

PERHAPS YOU HAVEN'T HEARD, SIR—GIVING HAS BEEN DECONTROLLED.

CHURCH AUDITORIUM

GOOD MORNING—COUGHING OR NON-COUGHING SECTION, PLEASE?

NATIONAL MAP

U.S. WEATHER BUREAU

COME ON, EDDIE—GO TO CHURCH WITH ME. THIS SUNDAY, THERE'S A 30 PERCENT CHANCE OF INSPIRATION.

PERHAPS YOU HAVEN'T HEARD, SIR—GIVING
HAS BEEN DECONTROLLED.

NOT ONLY IS HE A GREAT PASTOR, BUT HIS
RECENT SERMON ON TITHING IS BEING
PRINTED IN THE CONGRESSIONAL RECORD.

COME ON, EDDIE—GO TO CHURCH WITH ME.
THIS SUNDAY, THERE'S A 30 PERCENT
CHANCE OF INSPIRATION.

GOOD MORNING—COUGHING OR NON-
COUGHING SECTION, PLEASE?

I'LL BET THAT WAS ONE SERMON YOU'D LOVE TO HAVE BACK!

FRIENDS, AFTER THAT MOVIE, NO DOUBT YOU NEED SOME SPIRITUAL GUIDANCE. HERE IS REVEREND ED VOGELSANG.

OTHER PREACHERS USE COMMENTARIES TO GET UP SERMONS, BUT NO—YOU'RE TOO GOOD FOR THAT!

TELL YOU WHAT—YOU PRAY ABOUT THIS AND I'LL WHIP OFF A LETTER TO DEAR ABBY.

FRIENDS, AFTER THAT MOVIE, NO DOUBT
YOU NEED SOME SPIRITUAL GUIDANCE.
HERE IS REVEREND ED VOGELSANG.

I'LL BET THAT WAS ONE SERMON YOU'D
LOVE TO HAVE BACK!

OTHER PREACHERS USE COMMENTARIES TO
GET UP SERMONS, BUT NO—YOU'RE TOO
GOOD FOR THAT!

TELL YOU WHAT—YOU PRAY ABOUT THIS
AND I'LL WHIP OFF A LETTER TO DEAR ABBY.

AND WE THINK IT'S REALLY NEAT THE WAY YOU APPEAL TO YOUNG PEOPLE.

AND WE THINK IT'S REALLY NEAT THE WAY
YOU APPEAL TO YOUNG PEOPLE.

WHY WERE THE SHEPHERDS OUT WASHING THEIR SOCKS BY NIGHT?

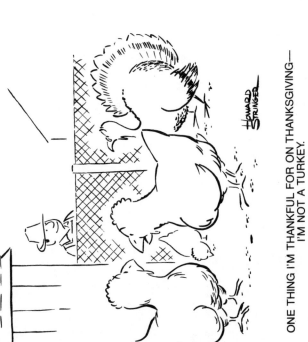

ONE THING I'M THANKFUL FOR ON THANKSGIVING—
I'M NOT A TURKEY.

MY MOM SAYS THERE'S NO WAY I CAN HAVE A DIRT BIKE, SO, I GUESS YOU BETTER MAKE IT A PONY INSTEAD.

YOU CAN COME UP NOW. THE GROUP VISITING FROM THE CHURCH HAS GONE.

ONE THING I'M THANKFUL FOR ON THANKSGIVING—
I'M NOT A TURKEY.

WHY WERE THE SHEPHERDS OUT WASHING THEIR
SOCKS BY NIGHT?

YOU CAN COME UP NOW. THE GROUP VISITING FROM
THE CHURCH HAS GONE.

MY MOM SAYS THERE'S NO WAY I CAN HAVE A DIRT
BIKE, SO, I GUESS YOU BETTER MAKE IT A PONY
INSTEAD.

LET'S HAVE LOCUST AN' WILD HONEY FOR LUNCH.

I THINK HE'S A LITTLE NERVOUS ABOUT BEING CALLED ON TO ASK THE OFFERTORY PRAYER.

WELL, PASTOR, YOU'RE CERTAINLY IN THE PROPER MOOD TO PREACH A "HELL FIRE AND BRIMSTONE" MESSAGE THIS SUNDAY MORNING.

WHY IS KING HEROD SO UPSET? WHAT DIFFERENCE CAN ONE LITTLE BABY MAKE?

I THINK HE'S A LITTLE NERVOUS ABOUT BEING CALLED ON TO ASK THE OFFERTORY PRAYER.

LET'S HAVE LOCUST AN' WILD HONEY FOR LUNCH.

WHY IS KING HEROD SO UPSET? WHAT DIFFERENCE CAN ONE LITTLE BABY MAKE?

WELL, PASTOR, YOU'RE CERTAINLY IN THE PROPER MOOD TO PREACH A "HELL FIRE AND BRIMSTONE" MESSAGE THIS SUNDAY MORNING.

WHAT YOU JUST READ IN TODAY'S PAPER SOUNDS EXACTLY LIKE WHAT I JUST READ ABOUT SODOM AND GOMORRAH.

IT WOULD BE JUST OUR LUCK FOR CHURCH TO BE RAPTURED NOW THAT WE'VE FINALLY PUT THE KIDS THROUGH COLLEGE AND PAID OFF THE MORTGAGE.

WITH THE AIR-CONDITIONING SYSTEM OUT, YOU YOUNG FELLOWS KNOW WHAT IT WAS LIKE TO GO TO CHURCH IN THE "GOOD OLD DAYS."

GOD THINKS I SHOULD SLEEP IN HERE 'TIL HE'S FINISHED MAKIN' IT THUNDER AN' LIGHTNIN'.

IT WOULD BE JUST OUR LUCK FOR CHURCH TO BE RAPTURED NOW THAT WE'VE FINALLY PUT THE KIDS THROUGH COLLEGE AND PAID OFF THE MORTGAGE.

WHAT YOU JUST READ IN TODAY'S PAPER SOUNDS EXACTLY LIKE WHAT I JUST READ ABOUT SODOM AND GOMORRAH.

GOD THINKS I SHOULD SLEEP IN HERE 'TIL HE'S FINISHED MAKIN' IT THUNDER AN' LIGHTNIN'.

WITH THE AIR-CONDITIONING SYSTEM OUT, YOU YOUNG FELLOWS KNOW WHAT IT WAS LIKE TO GO TO CHURCH IN THE "GOOD OLD DAYS."

TALK ABOUT SMART—HE EVEN KNOWS WHERE TO FIND ZEPHANIAH IN THE BIBLE.

READ US TH' STORY ABOUT TH' GUY WHO LET HIS GIRL FRIEND GIVE HIM A HAIRCUT.

DADDY DIDN'T HAVE TO STAND IN TH' CORNER WHEN HE SAID THAT WORD.

HOLD YOUR EARS FOR A MINUTE. I WANT TO TELL GOD A SECRET.

READ US TH' STORY ABOUT TH' GUY WHO LET HIS
GIRL FRIEND GIVE HIM A HAIRCUT.

TALK ABOUT SMART—HE EVEN KNOWS WHERE TO
FIND ZEPHANIAH IN THE BIBLE.

HOLD YOUR EARS FOR A MINUTE. I WANT TO TELL GOD
A SECRET.

DADDY DIDN'T HAVE TO STAND IN TH' CORNER WHEN
HE SAID THAT WORD.

IT WAS WORTH A TRY.

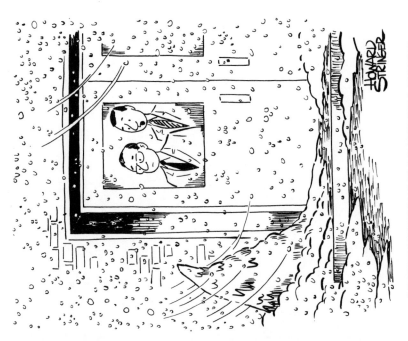

I DON'T THINK WE SHOULD EXPECT A RECORD ATTENDANCE THIS SUNDAY.

COULD WE HAVE A MOMENT OF PRAYER TOGETHER BEFORE YOU LOOK AT MY REPORT CARD?

JESUS DIDN'T HAV' TO WEAR A TIE TO CHURCH.

I DON'T THINK WE SHOULD EXPECT A RECORD
ATTENDANCE THIS SUNDAY.

IT WAS WORTH A TRY.

JESUS DIDN'T HAV' TO WEAR A TIE TO CHURCH.

COULD WE HAVE A MOMENT OF PRAYER TOGETHER
BEFORE YOU LOOK AT MY REPORT CARD?

I HEARD YOU SNICKER WHEN THE PREACHER TALKED ABOUT GOD KNOWING THE NUMBER OF HAIRS ON OUR HEADS.

MY SUNDAY SCHOOL TEACHER SAYS YOU SHOULD NEVER TELL A LIE.

I HOPE YOUR CHRISTIANITY IS STRONG ENOUGH TO
HANDLE A FLAT TIRE IN THE CHURCH PARKING LOT.

THERE CERTAINLY IS MORE OPENNESS AND HONESTY
IN THE CHURCH LATELY.

MY SUNDAY SCHOOL TEACHER SAYS YOU SHOULD <u>NEVER</u> TELL A LIE.

I HEARD YOU SNICKER WHEN THE PREACHER TALKED ABOUT GOD KNOWING THE NUMBER OF HAIRS ON OUR HEADS.

THERE CERTAINLY IS MORE OPENNESS AND HONESTY IN THE CHURCH LATELY.

I HOPE YOUR CHRISTIANITY IS STRONG ENOUGH TO HANDLE A FLAT TIRE IN THE CHURCH PARKING LOT.

CHURCH NURSERY

MRS. CRAWFORD SAYS YOU USED TO CRY WHEN YOU GOT LEFT IN THE NURSERY TOO.

I FEEL THIS IS A GOOD TIME TO ASK FOR A SPECIAL OFFERING TO REPLACE A BROKEN WINDOW.

WE'RE TRYIN' FOR PERFECT ATTENDANCE IN OUR SUNDAY SCHOOL...IF YOU MISS NEXT SUNDAY, I'LL PUNCH YOU IN TH' NOSE.

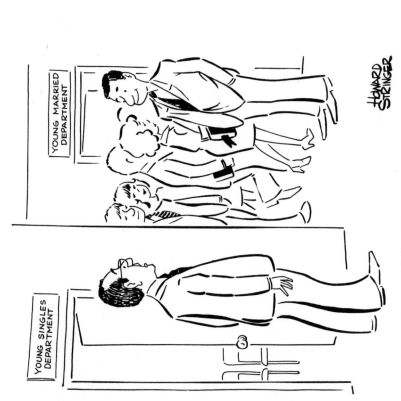

THIS RASH OF WEDDINGS IN THE CHURCH MAY BE GREAT FOR YOUR DEPARTMENT, BUT IT'S PLAYING HAVOC WITH MINE.

I FEEL THIS IS A GOOD TIME TO ASK FOR A SPECIAL OFFERING TO REPLACE A BROKEN WINDOW.

MRS. CRAWFORD SAYS YOU USED TO CRY WHEN YOU GOT LEFT IN THE NURSERY TOO.

THIS RASH OF WEDDINGS IN THE CHURCH MAY BE GREAT FOR YOUR DEPARTMENT, BUT IT'S PLAYING HAVOC WITH MINE.

WE'RE TRYIN' FOR PERFECT ATTENDANCE IN OUR SUNDAY SCHOOL...IF YOU MISS NEXT SUNDAY, I'LL PUNCH YOU IN TH' NOSE.

I KNOW WHAT'S IN THE BIBLE....MY GRANDMOTHER'S SECRET RECIPE FOR GERMAN CHOCOLATE CAKE.

DON'T GET YOUR CLOTHES DIRTY. THAT'S ALL YOU HAVE CLEAN TO WEAR TO CHURCH.

HE ALWAYS PREACHES HIS LONGEST SERMON WHEN THE FOOTBALL GAME STARTS EARLY.

WHICH ONE OF THESE CHURCH LADIES IS OL' MRS. HYPOCRITE, MAMA?

DON'T GET YOUR CLOTHES DIRTY. THAT'S ALL YOU
HAVE CLEAN TO WEAR TO CHURCH.

I KNOW WHAT'S IN THE BIBLE...MY GRANDMOTHER'S
SECRET RECIPE FOR GERMAN CHOCOLATE CAKE.

WHICH ONE OF THESE CHURCH LADIES IS OL' MRS.
HYPOCRITE, MAMA?

HE ALWAYS PREACHES HIS LONGEST SERMON WHEN
THE FOOTBALL GAME STARTS EARLY.

HOW MUCH LONGER DO I HAVE TO SIT PERFECTLY STILL?

OKAY IF I ACT NORMAL NOW THAT WE'RE OUT OF CHURCH?